PIANO
Adventures by Nancy and Randall Faber
Studio Collection

£3.99 20/2

This book belongs to: _____

Arranged by

Nancy and Randall Faber

Production Coordinator: Jon Ophoff
Design and Illustration: Terpstra Design, San Francisco
Engraving: Dovetree Productions, Inc.

FABER
PIANO ADVENTURES

3042 Creek Drive
Ann Arbor, Michigan 48108

A NOTE TO TEACHERS

The **Piano Adventures® Student Choice Series** offers an exciting set of arrangements in a variety of genres and at just the right level of difficulty.

This selection of **Level 6** pieces is designed to be fun, showy, and to inspire enthusiasm and pride in the intermediate piano student.

Invite your student to choose from additional styles in the series, each arranged at six levels, including:

- Popular
- Christmas
- Classics
- Studio Collection
- Jazz & Blues

Visit **www.PianoAdventures.com**

De **Piano Adventures® Student Choice Series** bevat fascinerende arrangementen in een keur aan stijlen, precies op het juiste niveau.

Met deze selectie van stukken in **niveau 6** kan de half gevorderde leerling zich met trots presenteren. Het is vooral plezierig, inspirerend en enthousiasmerend repertoire.

Er zijn arrangementen op 6 verschillende niveaus. Uw leerling kan kiezen uit vele stijlen, waaronder:

- Popular
- Christmas
- Classics
- Studio Collection
- Jazz & Blues

Bezoek ons op **www.PianoAdventures.nl**

La serie dei volumi **Student Choice** di **Piano Adventures®** offre una straordinaria gamma di arrangiamenti di diversi generi musicali e livelli di difficoltà.

La selezione del **Livello 6** è concepita per essere divertente e di grande impatto e per ispirare entusiasmo nell'allievo di livello intermedio.

Invita i tuoi studenti a scegliere tra gli altri stili proposti dalla serie, ognuno dei quali è arrangiato a sei livelli di difficoltà e comprende:

- Pop
- Natale
- Classici
- Studio Collection
- Jazz & Blues

Visita **www.PianoAdventures.it**

Die Hefte der Reihe **Student Choice Series** von **Piano Adventures®** bieten anregende Arrangements im passenden Schwierigkeitsgrad und in unterschiedlichen Stilrichtungen.

Stufe 6: Mit dieser Auswahl an Stücken kann sich der nun leicht fortgeschrittene Schüler mit Stolz und Bravour präsentieren. Dies inspiriert und macht Spaß zugleich.

Lassen Sie Ihre Schüler aus den folgenden jeweils in sechs Stufen vorliegenden Heften wählen:

- Popular
- Christmas
- Classics
- Studio Collection
- Jazz & Blues

Besuchen Sie uns: **www.PianoAdventures.de**

La **serie de libros suplementarios "Student Choice"** de **Piano Adventures®** ofrece adaptaciones de piezas cautivadoras en una gran variedad de géneros y niveles de dificultad.

Las piezas divertidas y llamativas del **Nivel 6** despiertan el entusiasmo y el orgullo de los estudiantes de nivel intermedio temprano.

Invite a sus estudiantes a elegir entre los siguientes estilos, cada uno disponible en seis niveles:

- Popular
- Navidad
- Clásicos
- *Studio Collection*
- *Jazz* y *Blues*

Para más información, visite **www.PianoAdventures-es.com**

IEFF302

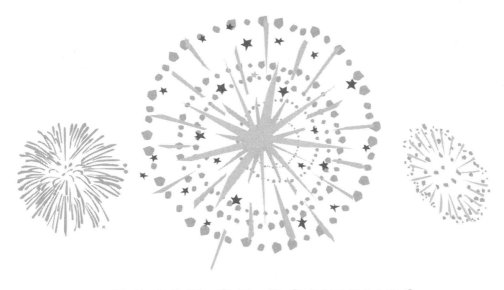

TABLE OF CONTENTS

Canon in D. 4

The Pink Panther 8

Can You Feel the Love Tonight (from *The Lion King*). . .12

Morning Has Broken 15

Rock Around the Clock. .18

100 Years. 22

Autumn Leaves 26

Deep River. 29

Solace. 32

Gangnam Style. 36

Music Dictionary 41

Canon in D

JOHANN PACHELBEL
(1653-1706)

IEFF30

The Pink Panther

from *THE PINK PANTHER*

Music by
HENRY MANCINI

IEFF30

Can You Feel the Love Tonight

from Walt Disney's *The Lion King*

Music by ELTON JOHN
Lyrics by TIM RICE

IEFF302

Additional Lyrics

There's a time for everyone, if they only learn
That the twisting kaleidoscope moves us all in turn.
There's a rhyme and reason to the wild outdoors
When the heart of this star-crossed voyager beats in time with yours. *To Chorus*

Morning Has Broken

TRADITIONAL

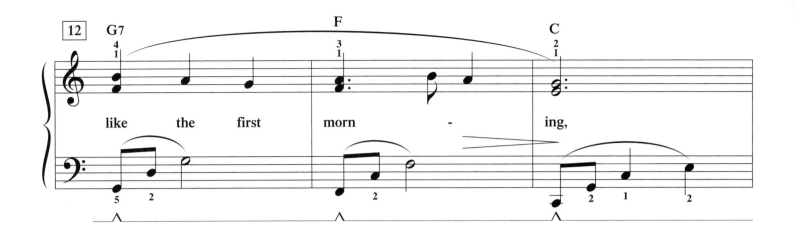

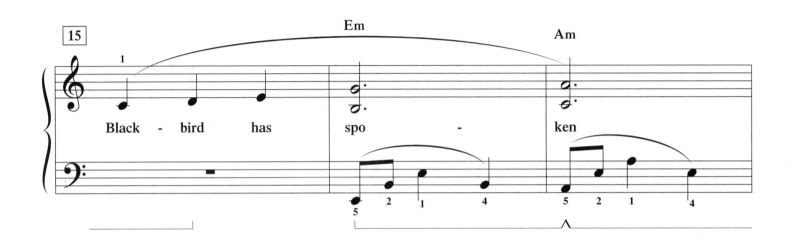

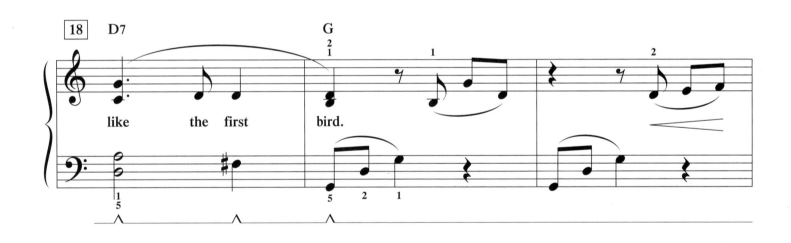

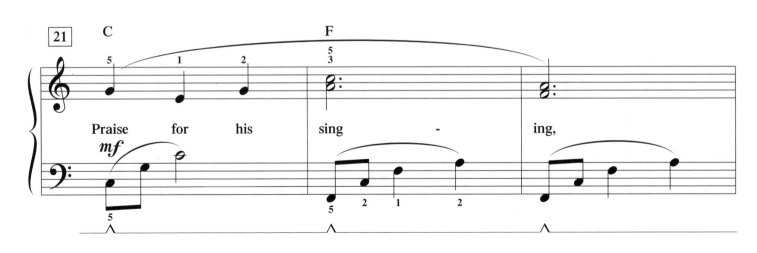

Rock Around the Clock

Words by
MAX C. FREEDMAN

Music by
JIMMY DeKNIGHT

Fast Swing

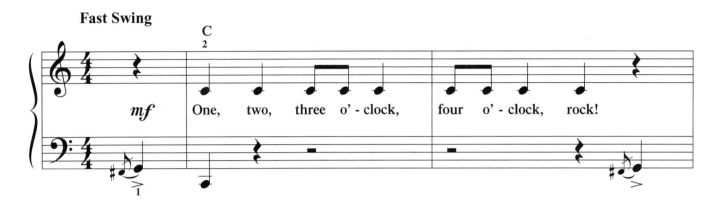

One, two, three o'- clock, four o'- clock, rock!

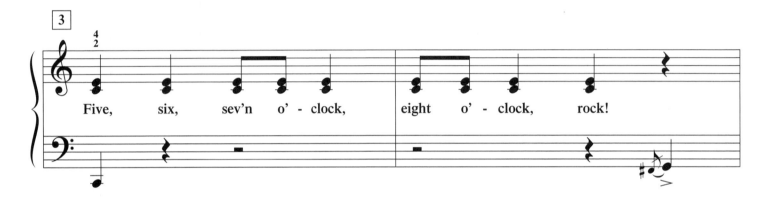

Five, six, sev'n o'- clock, eight o'- clock, rock!

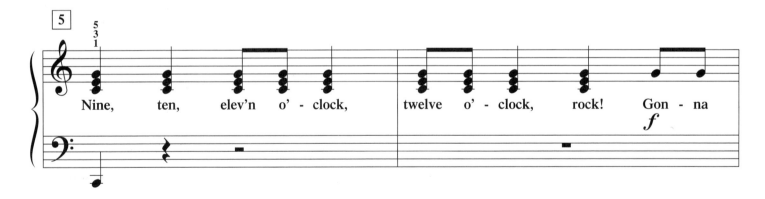

Nine, ten, elev'n o'- clock, twelve o'- clock, rock! Gon - na

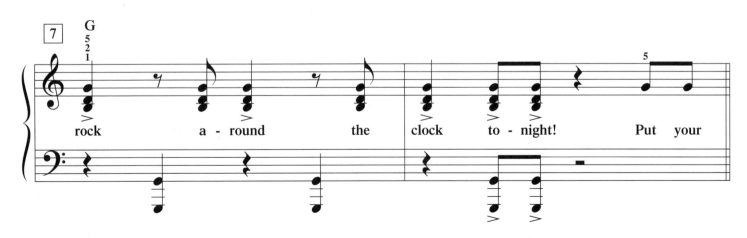

rock a - round the clock to - night! Put your

IEFF302

100 Years

Words and Music by
JOHN ONDRASIK

I'm fif - teen___ for a mo - ment,___
I'm twen - ty - two for a mo - ment,___

caught up___ be - tween ten and twen - ty and I'm just___ dream -
and she___ feels bet - ter than ev - er and we're on___ fire,

IEFF302

Autumn Leaves

English lyrics by JOHNNY MERCER
French lyrics by JACQUES PREVERT

Music by
JOSEPH KOSMA

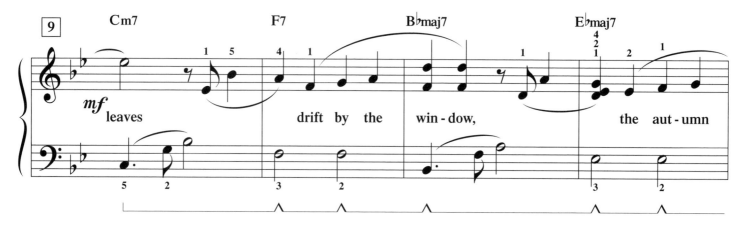

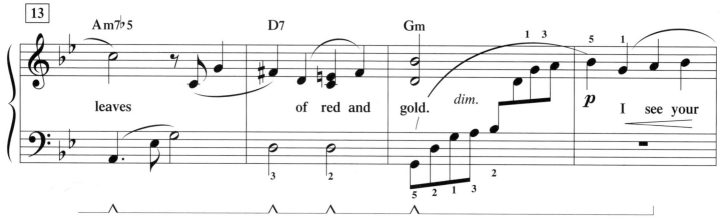

IEFF302

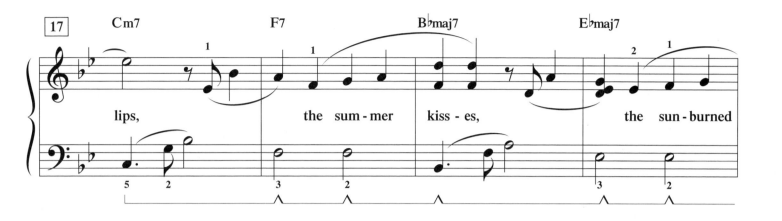

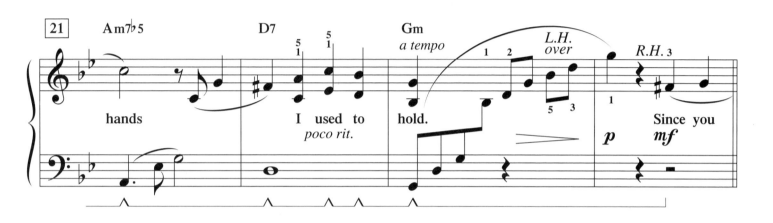

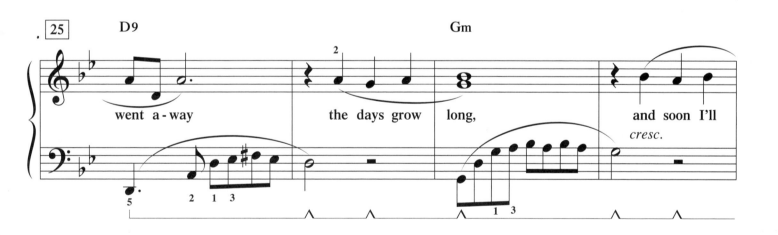

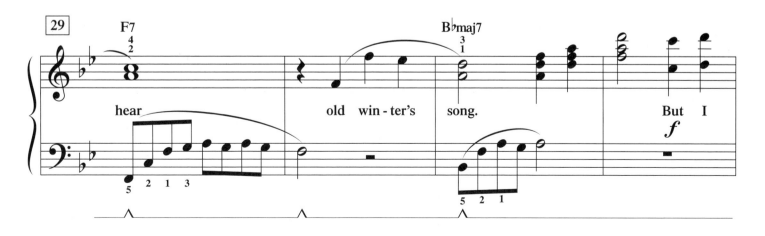

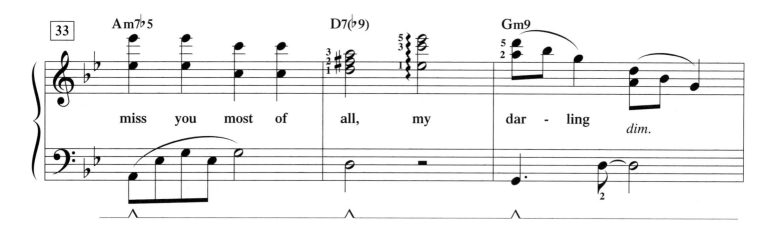

miss you most of all, my dar - ling *dim.*

when au - tumn leaves start to

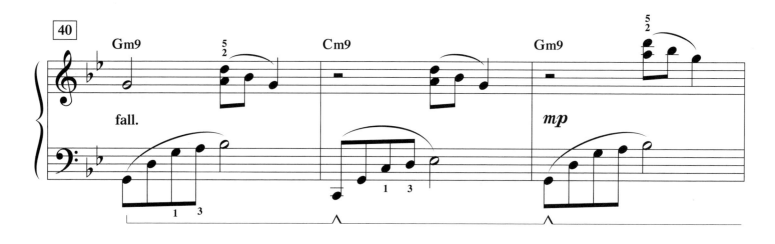

fall.

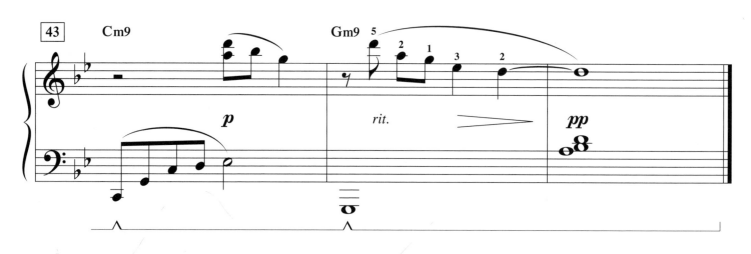

Deep River

Solace

SCOTT JOPLIN

Very slow march time (♩ = 80-84)

IEFF30

Gangnam Style

Words and Music by
GUN HYUNG YOO and JAI SANG PARK

IEFF30